Remembering
Columbus

Nick Taggart

TURNER
PUBLISHING COMPANY

An aerial view of Columbus looking west in 1965.

Remembering
Columbus

Turner Publishing Company
www.turnerpublishing.com

Remembering Columbus

Copyright © 2010 Turner Publishing Company

Library of Congress Control Number: 2010923492

ISBN: 978-1-59652-621-1

Printed in the United States of America

ISBN: 978-1-68336-821-2 (pbk.)

Contents

The former Franklin County Courthouse was photographed shortly after it was completed in 1887. It occupied the southeast corner of High and Mound streets. George Bellows, Sr., father of the famous artist, was the Superintendent of Construction.

Acknowledgments

This volume, *Remembering Columbus,* is the result of the cooperation and efforts of many individuals and organizations.

It takes a community to preserve local history, especially visual history. The photographs featured in this book come from the "Columbus in Historic Photographs" collection, maintained by the Biography, History, and Travel Division of the Columbus Metropolitan Library. This archive of images has been collected over time from a variety of sources, not the least of which have been interested members of the general public. It is through the combined efforts of individuals that our collective history is preserved.

This volume would not have been possible without the professional and amateur historians devoted to preserving the past, including the dedicated staff—past and present—of the Biography, History, and Travel Division of the Columbus Metropolitan Library.

The writer also wishes to acknowledge and thank his wife, Michele, for her suggestions and editing skills. Her contributions have made this a better book.

The publisher would like to thank Nick Taggart, the writer, for his valuable contributions and assistance in making this work possible.

PREFACE

Columbus has thousands of historic photographs that reside in archives, both locally and nationally. This book began with the observation that, while those photographs are of great interest to many, they are not easily accessible. During a time when Columbus is looking ahead and evaluating its future course, many people are asking, How do we treat the past? These decisions affect every aspect of the city—architecture, public spaces, commerce, infrastructure—and these, in turn, affect the way that people live their lives. This book seeks to provide easy access to a valuable, objective look into the history of Columbus.

The power of photographs is that they are less subjective than words in their treatment of history. Although the photographer can make subjective decisions regarding subject matter and how to capture and present it, photographs seldom interpret the past to the extent textual histories can. For this reason, photography is uniquely positioned to offer an original, untainted look at the past, allowing the viewer to learn for himself what the world was like a century or more ago.

This project represents countless hours of review and research. The researchers and writer have reviewed thousands of photographs in numerous archives. We greatly appreciate the generous assistance of those listed in the acknowledgments of this work, without whom this project could not have been completed.

The goal in publishing this work is to provide broader access to this set of extraordinary photographs, which seek to inspire, provide perspective, and evoke insight that might assist people who are responsible for determining Columbus's future. In addition, the book seeks to preserve the past with adequate respect and reverence.

With the exception of touching up imperfections that have accrued with the passage of time and cropping where necessary, no changes have been made. The focus and clarity of many images are limited to the technology and the ability of the photographer at the time they were recorded.

The work is divided into eras. Beginning with some of the earliest known photographs of Columbus, the first section records photographs from the Civil War era through the late nineteenth century. The second section spans the years 1898 to 1913. Section Three moves from 1914 to the beginning of the Great Depression era. The last section covers the 1930s to 1960s.

In each of these sections we have made an effort to capture various aspects of life through our selection of photographs. People, commerce, transportation, infrastructure, religious institutions, and educational institutions have been included to provide a broad perspective.

We encourage readers to reflect as they go walking in Columbus, strolling through the city, its parks, and its neighborhoods. It is the publisher's hope that in utilizing this work, longtime residents will learn something new and that new residents will gain a perspective on where Columbus has been, so that each can contribute to its future.

—*Todd Bottorff, Publisher*

The first passenger rail service running in and out of the city was the Columbus and Xenia in 1850. This wooden structure was the city's first railway station. Located at what was then the northernmost end of High Street, it served for a quarter of a century before a new depot was built in 1875.

Born to Be the Capital

(1860s–1897)

Broad Street looking east from High Street, circa 1875. Businesses included a jewelry store, several groceries, the Columbus Business College, and the Buckeye House, a popular hotel.

Tanneries could be foul-smelling places, but they provided important leather products. The Buchsieb Tannery, at 419 South Front Street, was a successful nineteenth-century Columbus business. It was founded in 1848.

Patrick Egan began his Undertaking and Livery business in 1859. The establishment was only five years old when this photograph was taken on West Naghten Street. The company continues today as Egan-Ryan Funeral Service.

In 1867, only three firehouses provided service to the city of Columbus. This is the Third Street Engine House, located on the southwest corner with Chapel Street. Its crew proudly displays its horse-drawn ladder cart.

This 1868 view of State Street, just west of High Street, features the George Norris Company, a seller of soda and mineral water.

The George Bauer Bakery was located at 185 South Fourth Street in 1882, when its staff posed for this picture. The bakery was in business from 1865 to 1937.

The massive Centennial Auditorium was built on the fairgrounds especially for the celebration. It could seat more than 10,000 people and its acoustics were said to be so perfect that a whisper could be heard all around the interior. Despite its $12,000 construction cost, it was intended as a temporary structure and razed shortly after the close of events.

A train leaves Union Station under a wooden viaduct. The viaduct was a temporary walkway constructed for the G.A.R. National Encampment in 1888.

The Monypeny Block was built in 1878 and expanded in 1884 to include the entire eastside block of High Street from Long Street to Lafayette Street. It was demolished in 1970.

There isn't a parking lot in sight in this 1889 view of High Street looking north from Gay Street.

The grounds of the Columbus Barracks in 1889. The area went by many names and served many military purposes over the years. It began in 1864 as a Civil War arsenal. During World War I, it was a recruiting depot. Later, under the name Fort Hayes, it was the headquarters of the U.S. Army's Fifth Corps. It is currently home to the Columbus Public School's Fort Hayes Metropolitan Education Center.

This is an 1889 view of Broad Street looking east from High Street. The Hayden Clinton Bank, third building from the left, was built in 1869 and is currently the oldest structure on the square surrounding the Ohio Statehouse.

The second Union Station in 1889. This brick and stone structure was built in 1875 to replace its wooden predecessor. It sheltered an impressive seven sets of tracks, but was razed in 1896 to make way for a more modern train station.

This 1889 view looking north was taken from the hub of Columbus, the intersection of Broad and High streets.

The Streetcar Strike of 1890 lasted for one week in June. This photograph shows strike sympathizers removing a streetcar from the Long Street line and placing it crosswise at the intersection of Long and High streets. The strike ended when both sides agreed to an increase in wages and a reduction of the workday from 16 to 12 hours.

Employees at the Columbus Watch Company in 1890. Located at 79 East Thurman Avenue, the company produced watches in the city for 30 years beginning in 1883.

The crew takes a break from building the Mound Street Bridge. The man at left is Chester Melvin Davis, a stonemason from Indiana—and the writer's great-grandfather.

After Civil War general and Ohio native William Tecumseh Sherman died in 1891, his funeral train paused in Columbus on its way to St. Louis, Missouri. The train was met at Union Station by a throng of 10,000, including two regiments of the Ohio National Guard and a committee of Ohio legislators.

One of the most spectacular fires in the city's history broke out on the evening of November 24, 1893, when half a block bounded by High, Spring, and Front streets, and Hickory Alley, went up in flames. The Chittenden Hotel, the Chittenden Hall, and the Henrietta and Park theaters were completely destroyed. The Chittenden Hotel was later rebuilt with fireproof material.

The rebuilt Chittenden Hotel during construction of the electric streetcar lines.

The employees of the J. W. Martin Printing Company take a break outside their office at 40 West Town Street. The firm worked from this location in the mid-1890s and promised "book and job printing promptly and neatly executed."

Family and friends gathered outside the Elizabeth Ross Grocery in 1896. It was located at 854 North Fourth Street, on the southeast corner with First Avenue.

The Sheridan Brothers Blacksmith Shop, at 406 West State Street, was in business from about 1897 to 1904.

Electric streetcars and horse-drawn vehicles were sharing the road by 1897. This view includes the Park Hotel at the northwest corner of Goodale and North High streets.

Blacksmith John S. McClellan worked out of a shop on South Front Street in the 1890s.

This 1897 photograph was taken from the Wheeler Building on West Broad Street and looks down on North High Street. The banner at the bottom of the picture promotes the Ohio State Fair, which was held for four days that year.

With the Ohio State Fair in progress, this street level view looking north up High Street shows the late-nineteenth-century hustle and bustle of downtown Columbus.

Where's the fire? These Columbus firemen certainly know as they race along East Broad Street in their horse-drawn fire engine. The First Congregational Church, at 74 East Broad Street, is visible in the background.

The beautiful Board of Trade
Building graced East Broad Street,
across from the statehouse, for
80 years. It was razed in 1969 to
make way for the Rhodes State
Office Tower.

The Arsenal Building at the United States Barracks in 1897. The Arsenal was built in 1864 at a cost of $42,375. It was a storehouse for arms and other military material.

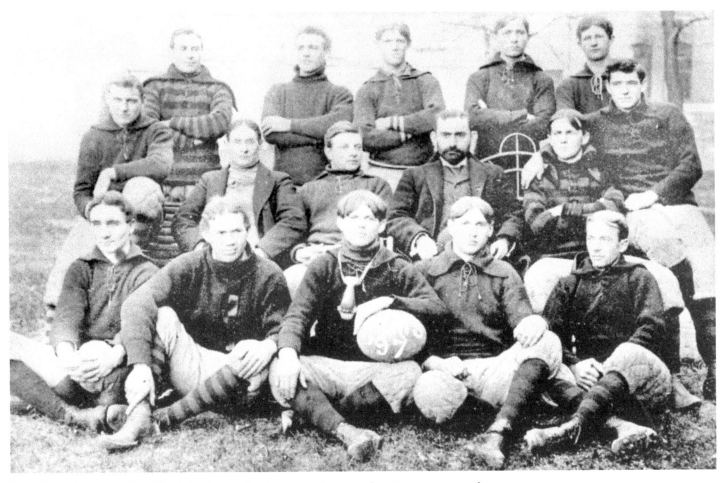

The Alerts, the 1897 Ohio School for the Deaf rugby team. They scored against every team they played that year and defeated several of them.

Myron Trope, a Russian immigrant, ran a grocery store that doubled as a saloon. In 1897, his business was at 2575 North High Street.

Seen here in 1897, this building served as the Columbus prison and police headquarters for 40 years, until 1920. It was located on the northwest corner of Town and Scioto streets, the latter now known as Civic Center Drive.

In 1896, the Grant Memorial Building was constructed around the cottage where President Ulysses Grant was born, in order to protect it. President McKinley is seen here visiting the memorial during the 1897 Ohio State Fair.

A call to arms came in 1898 as a result of the Spanish-American War. Camp Bushnell was created east of Columbus where the suburb of Bexley now stands. Pedestrians and cyclists are seen here near the East Broad Street entrance to the camp.

BETWEEN THE FLOODS
(1898–1913)

On May 15, 1898, cannons on the statehouse grounds boomed as the Fourth Ohio Volunteer Infantry paraded past, on their way from Camp Bushnell to Union Station.

Prisoners and a guard stand outside the gate of the Ohio Penitentiary on Spring Street.

The Columbus Buggy Company once claimed to be the largest buggy manufacturer in the world, turning out one vehicle every eight minutes. The firm began business as the Iron Buggy Company in this unassuming building at 180 North High Street.

The city's third Union Station was completed in 1897. A viaduct carried North High Street over the tracks. In April of 1898, the Columbus Shriners paraded south on High Street with elephants and camels they borrowed from the Sells Brothers Circus.

This is what the block of South High Street across from the statehouse looked like at the start of the twentieth century. The building with the marquee is the Goodale Hotel and next to it to the north is the Ambos Restaurant.

The days of the horse and buggy were numbered in 1902, when this photograph of East Broad Street was taken.

Hardesty Brothers, 304-310 West Mound Street, was a milling company that operated from 1880 to 1927. Its brands of flour included Purity, White Frost, and Paragon.

High Street looking north from near Gay Street in 1902.

University Hall, seen here in 1903, served Ohio State University for nearly a century. Construction of this campus oval landmark was completed in 1873. The building was razed in 1970 to make way for a second University Hall, a near replica of the first.

Not much remained after an April 26, 1903, fire destroyed the Union Department Store and other businesses at the northwest corner of High and Long streets. A Columbus fire fighter, Captain Daniel S. Lewis, lost his life while battling the blaze.

St. Anthony's Hospital, 1450 Hawthorne Avenue, in 1903. The building was dedicated in 1891 and served the residents of the east side of Columbus until its demolition in 1970.

The manner of dress might have been different, but the Ohio state fair was as popular in 1903 as it is today. More than 74,000 visitors attended the 5-day exposition that year and were entertained by agricultural exhibits, a Wild West show, and a life-size butter cow.

The Masonic Temple, 34 North Fourth Street, is seen here five years after construction in 1898. An addition was built in 1935, more than doubling the structure's size. Saved from demolition in the 1990s, the building now provides convention and meeting space under the name Columbus Athenaeum.

A delivery wagon for the Jeffrey Manufacturing Company in 1904. In the early twentieth century, the company was a national leader in mining equipment manufacturing.

Scott Krauss, left, opened his news agency at 654 North High Street on February 15, 1903.

Heber Brothers was a family affair that operated for ten years. Pictured here are George T. Heber (with trombone), Reginald F. Heber (with trumpet, near horse), Avanell C. Heber Cramer (in a kilt at left of platform), Abbie Rose Heber (behind dog), and Rose Heber Mckinney (seated at right-center).

Heber Brothers Shows was a traveling circus with its headquarters at 288 East Seventeenth Avenue. Mr. and Mrs. George Heber are shown here in 1907 with one of the show's 27 wagons.

The Columbus Ice and Cold Storage Company was incorporated in 1898. Located at 219 Spruce Street, it boasted having the state's first plate ice factory. The cake of ice seen here is 9.5 feet wide, 13.5 feet long, and 11 inches thick.

The first Columbus Public Library was located in the old City Hall building on State Street. Thanks to an initial $200,000 gift from Andrew Carnegie, the city was able to build this beautiful structure at 96 South Grant Avenue. It was dedicated in 1907. In a generous act of payback, the library served as a temporary city hall when the State Street building was destroyed by fire in 1921.

President William McKinley, a former Ohio governor, was assassinated in 1901 while attending the Pan-American Exposition in Buffalo, New York. This monument in front of the Ohio Statehouse was dedicated on September 14, 1906, and portrays the president speaking at the exposition.

The Ohio Penitentiary, circa 1900. For better or worse, the Pen was a Columbus landmark for more than 160 years. Facing Spring Street and sprawling back along Neil Avenue, it encompassed 23 acres. It ceased housing prisoners in 1984. The last of its buildings were demolished in 1998, making way for development of the Arena District.

The Columbus Dispatch Building, at the northeast corner of High and Gay streets, was destroyed by fire April 9, 1907.

The Camp Chase streetcar in front of the Camp Chase Post Office on Broad Street west of Hague Avenue.

The High Street arches are decorated with patriotic bunting in this 1908 photograph looking north from Vine Street.

Residents take a rest on the McKinley Monument, along the High Street side of the Ohio Statehouse, in 1908.

Franklinton neighborhood in 1908. An impressive city plan for Columbus was unveiled in 1908. It included ideas for linking both sides of the Scioto River by improving riverfront properties and deteriorating neighborhoods such as this one in Franklinton. Much of the plan was never implemented.

Sometimes known as the Old Old Post Office, this beautiful building on the southeast corner of Third and State streets opened in 1887. It served as a post office and United States courthouse. Soon after this 1908 photograph was taken, the building was enlarged, doubling its size. It currently serves as the law offices of Brickler and Eckler.

Columbus City Hall on State Street in 1908. Before this building was completed in 1872, local government business was conducted on the second floor of the old Central Market House. City Hall was destroyed by fire in 1921. The site is now occupied by the Ohio Theater.

Columbus native Elsie Janis christened the hot-air balloon *Iroquois* on August 26, 1908. Janis was a popular singer and actress. The *Iroquois* was Columbus's entrant in a balloon race that began at Driving Park three days later.

Automobiles were becoming more prevalent by the time this post-1913 photograph was taken at the intersection of Broad and High streets.

It's bumper-to-bumper parking on Gay Street in this view looking east from High Street.

J. Q. Hartsough & Company, a dry goods store at 1240 West Broad Street, 1910.

The southern end of downtown is featured in this 1910 view of High Street looking north from Fulton Street.

Everyone loves a parade and the North High Street viaduct was crowded with onlookers in this 1910 photograph.

This 1910 scene looking north from the intersection of Broad and High streets features an array of transportation modes including a horse and buggy, streetcar, automobile, and good old-fashioned legs.

Construction of the Toledo and Ohio Central Railroad Depot's elevated tracks in 1911.

The 1912 Ohio-Columbus Centennial Celebration kicked off on August 26 with a parade reflecting the city's leading industries. This float belonged to the Max H. Rieser Company, 66 East Main Street, a producer of men's and women's wear.

The Ohio-Columbus Centennial Celebration ran from August 26 to September 1, 1912. Each day was filled with a variety of events including parades, exhibitions, and fireworks.

Folks wait outside the Billy Sunday Tabernacle, 570 North Park Street, in 1913. The famous evangelist held services in Columbus for seven weeks, concluding on February 16, 1913. On the last day, Sunday preached to more than 39,000 people at four services.

The Flood of 1913 was devastating for Columbus. More than $5.5 million in property damage was reported and 93 people lost their lives.

A bread line for 1913 Flood victims. In the first days after the flood, 20,000 people were fed from relief supplies.

Looking north on High Street from Gay Street in 1913.

This double-deck J. G. Brill streetcar #1000 could hold 81 passengers. It began service on the High Street line on February 24, 1914, but lasted only one year.

GOOD OLD COLUMBUS TOWN

(1914–1930)

Exhibition race, June 6-7, 1914. Pilot Lincoln Beachey and auto racer Barney Oldfield competed in a two-day speed contest at the Driving Park Racetrack. The airplane was first around the one-mile course on the first day; the automobile was the winner on the second day.

While crossing the finish line 10 feet ahead of Beachey on the second day, Oldfield also set a new one-mile course record. His 100-horsepower Fiat completed the route in 49 seconds.

The Jeffrey Manufacturing Company's employee choral society sponsored a May festival at Olentangy Park on May 22, 1915. The company offered many employee programs and benefits, establishing it as a good place to work.

The Ford Motor Company, 427 Cleveland Avenue, had been open a year when this photograph was taken in 1915. It operated until 1939, and the building later became part of the Kroger Bakery.

The Dodson Sawmill and Lumber Company, 555 Cleveland Avenue, in 1915.

Looking northwest toward Broad and High streets from the Statehouse in 1916. The larger buildings in the picture include the Harrison Building housing the Huntington National Bank (far left), the Deshler Hotel (center), and the State Savings and Trust and New Hayden buildings (far right).

A pedestrian's view of High Street in 1916, looking north from the Ohio Statehouse.

Looking west on Broad Street from the Statehouse grounds in 1916.

An early form of traffic control is featured in this 1916 scene on High Street looking north from Gay Street.

The east bank of the Scioto River near the Broad Street Bridge was crowded with industrial sites and slums, circa 1916.

The Red Cross float in a patriotic parade held in downtown Columbus on June 9, 1918. Twenty-five thousand people participated in a show of support for the American troops in World War I.

Former President Theodore Roosevelt visited Columbus on September 30, 1918. Roosevelt dedicated a memorial arch at Broad and High streets to the first 43 men of Franklin County who died during World War I.

The Armistice Day celebration along North High Street on November 11, 1918, marked the
conclusion of World War I.

Many Columbus businesses closed on April 6, 1919, so that employees could attend the parades. The Jeffrey Manufacturing Company welcomed Batteries A, B, and C of the 37th Division, which included many former employees. The company restaurant served meals to many of the returning soldiers.

The Toledo and Ohio Central Railroad Depot, at 379 West Broad Street, in 1919. This view looks north along the elevated platform tracks from the rear of the depot.

Motormen pose next to the High Street streetcar no. 625 in 1921. The front of the car advertises the latest moving-picture show at B. F. Keith's Theatre.

Guy Denton in his grocery store at 686 Parsons Avenue, circa 1920. Most items were stacked behind the counter and had to be retrieved for customers by a clerk.

Construction of Ohio Stadium in 1922. The pride of the Ohio State University, the double-deck "Horseshoe" was the first of its kind in the country. Dedicated on October 21, 1922, the facility could seat 63,000 people.

The east side of High Street looking north from Lafayette Street in 1925. The stores featured in the photograph include the Armbruster Company, Bartlett's Clothing, and the Boston Store.

Charles Lindbergh met with Columbus Airport Commission members at Norton Field, 4321 East Broad Street, on October 22, 1928. His visit was in support of the proposed airport that would become Port Columbus.

Acrophobes need not apply. A laborer pauses, suspended high above Columbus from atop the AIU Citadel in 1929.

THE ALL AMERICAN CITY
(1931–1960s)

Looking southeast toward the new Civic Center along the banks of the Scioto River in 1933. The United States Post Office and Courthouse (left), the Columbus City Hall (center), and the Ohio Departments of State Building (right) were all built within a span of six years.

Broad Street at Grant Avenue circa 1931 featured tree-lined parkways. Looking east, the Ohio State Life Insurance Company building is at left and the Seneca Hotel is at right.

A sheep-shearing competition at the Ohio state fair.

The Rocky Fork Country Club, 5189 Clark State Road, held its annual Hunters Trail on November 7, 1931.

Studio car no. 7, "a gigantic studio on wheels," produced by the Mercier Amplifier and Equipment Company. The firm operated from 1929 to 1978 and offered portable public sound systems.

The southeast corner of High and State streets saw a lot of foot traffic in 1940. Businesses included Hall and Steel Shoe Repair, the Fanny Farmer Candy Shop, and the Foot Saver Shoe Shop.

A military color guard leads a parade down Broad Street between Third and High streets.

Looking southeast across the intersection of Broad and High streets in 1945. The Deshler-Wallick Hotel sat on the northwest corner, across West Broad Street from the Adam Hat Shop. The Statehouse dominates the city center while above the trees to the far left is seen the bell tower of Trinity Episcopal Church.

Rail fans took a ride along East Chestnut Street on a Sunday in August 1948.

Columbus's last electric streetcar running along Neil Avenue on September 4, 1948. The first electric car had been exhibited during the 1888 Ohio State Fair. It replaced the horse-drawn trolley, which bowed out of service in 1892.

General Dwight Eisenhower's presidential campaign swept through Columbus on September 24, 1952. He is seen here with his wife, Mamie, and Robert A. Taft. Eisenhower won Ohio and the presidency.

Fans head toward Ohio Stadium on an autumn day in 1952. The Buckeyes went 6-3 that year with a satisfying 27–7 win over Michigan. The team included freshman Howard Cassady, who would win the Heisman Trophy three years later.

A horse-drawn fruit cart makes an early morning delivery to Central Market on South Fourth Street.

The Ohio Theatre, at 39 East State Street, in 1955. The marquee advertises *Davy Crocket, Indian Scout,* starring George Montgomery.

This view of Broad and High streets in 1955 features the LeVeque Lincoln Tower and the RKO Palace Theatre, the Deshler-Hilton Hotel, and Roy's Jewelers.

Looking east at Columbus City Hall in 1955. The City Hall Annex is to the left and the lower floors of the LeVeque Tower are visible on the right.

The Columbus Dispatch Building, 34 South Third Street, in 1955. The newspaper began publishing in 1871 and has been open at this location since 1925.

The Christopher Columbus statue dedication in front of City Hall on October 12, 1955. The 20-foot bronze statue, sculptured by Edoardo Alfieri, was a gift from the citizens of Genoa, Italy. A crowd of nearly 100,000 people followed the Columbus Day parade to City Hall before the official unveiling.

For nearly a century and a half, a Neil House hotel faced the Ohio Statehouse across High Street. Shown here in 1955 is the third building to have displayed that name. The hotel closed in 1980 and was razed to make room for the Huntington Bank Center.

The Ohio State Buckeyes capped the 1958 football season on November 22 with a 20–14 victory over the Michigan Wolverines. The team finished with a record of 6-1-2.

The *General,* a century-old locomotive, pulled into Union Station on May 2, 1962, as part of the National Civil War Centennial Observance. One hundred years earlier, a group of Union soldiers from Ohio had captured the *General* from the Confederate Army in Georgia.

The Rowland Building on the northeast corner of High and Third streets, circa 1962. Shown under construction to the north is the Sheraton Plaza.

Looking south on High Street from near Elm Street. Kay Jewelers, 68 North High Street, was located in the historic Hinman-Beatty Block, which dated to the nineteenth century.

Senator Barry Goldwater visited Columbus on September 30, 1964, while campaigning for president. An estimated 10,000 people came out to hear him speak from the veranda of Veterans Memorial on West Broad Street.

The Civic Center lights reflect off the Scioto River in this nighttime view from 1968.

The west side of High Street, south of Lynn Alley, in 1969. The Deshler Hotel (center-left) was demolished the following year. The Annex Block (center-right) was destroyed by fire in 1974.

An aerial view of downtown Columbus looking east in 1969.

NOTES ON THE PHOTOGRAPHS

These notes, listed by page number, attempt to include all aspects known of the photographs. Each of the photographs is identified by the page number, a title or description, photographer and collection, archive, and call or box number when applicable. Although every attempt was made to collect all data, in some cases complete data may have been unavailable due to the age and condition of some of the photographs and records.

41 UNION STATION AND VIADUCT
Columbus Metropolitan Library
CCVC# 786/00/1898

42 SOUTH HIGH LOOKING NORTH
Columbus Metropolitan Library
CCVC# 880/00/1900/01

43 EAST BROAD STREET
Columbus Metropolitan Library
CCVC# 883/00/1902

44 HARDESTY BROTHERS MILLERS
Columbus Metropolitan Library
CCVC# 272/H259/1901

45 HIGH STREET NEAR GAY STREET
Columbus Metropolitan Library
CCVC# 888/00/1902

46 UNIVERSITY HALL
Columbus Metropolitan Library
CCVC# 701/U58/1903

47 UNION DEPARTMENT STORE FIRE
Columbus Metropolitan Library
CCVC# 470/U58/1903

48 ST. ANTHONY'S HOSPITAL
Columbus Metropolitan Library
CCVC# 565/00/1903

49 OHIO STATE FAIR AT THE TURN OF THE CENTURY
Columbus Metropolitan Library
CCVC# 456/G882/1903

50 MASONIC TEMPLE
Columbus Metropolitan Library
CCVC# 080/M399/1903

51 JEFFREY MANUFACTURING COMPANY DELIVERY WAGON
Columbus Metropolitan Library
CCVC# 911/J46/1904

52 SCOTT KRAUSS NEWS AGENCY
Columbus Metropolitan Library
CCVC# 272/K91/1903

53 HEBER BROTHERS CIRCUS TENT WITH BAND
Columbus Metropolitan Library
CCVC# 360/H445/1907

54 HEBER BROTHERS SHOWS
Columbus Metropolitan Library
CCVC# 360/H445/1907/01

55 COLUMBUS ICE AND COLD STORAGE
Columbus Metropolitan Library
CCVC# 272/I15/1901/01

56 COLUMBUS PUBLIC LIBRARY
Columbus Metropolitan Library
CCVC# 628/00/00/33

57 McKINLEY MONUMENT
Columbus Metropolitan Library
CCVC# 667/M158/1908/03

58 OHIO PENITENTIARY
Columbus Metropolitan Library
CCVC# 776/P411/1900/01

59 DISPATCH BUILDING FIRE
Columbus Metropolitan Library
CCVC# 470/D612/1907

60 CAMP CHASE STREETCAR
Columbus Metropolitan Library
CCVC# 671/C487

61 NORTH HIGH STREET LOOKING NORTH FROM VINE STREET
Columbus Metropolitan Library
CCVC# 888/V782/1908/01

62 McKINLEY MONUMENT
Columbus Metropolitan Library
CCVC# 667/M158/1908/01

63 FRANKLINTON NEIGHBORHOOD
Columbus Metropolitan Library
CCVC# 892/F831/1908

64 OLD OLD POST OFFICE
Columbus Metropolitan Library
CCVC# 177/00/1908

65 CITY HALL
Columbus Metropolitan Library
CCVC# 113/00/1908

66 ELSIE JANIS
Columbus Metropolitan Library
CCVC# 094/J33/1908

67 STREETCAR AT BROAD AND HIGH
Columbus Metropolitan Library
CCVC# 885/H638

95 RETURNING
SOLDIERS
Columbus Metropolitan
Library
CCVC# 674/00/1919/02

96 TOLEDO AND OHIO
CENTRAL RAILROAD
DEPOT
Columbus Metropolitan
Library
CCVC# 783/T649/1919/01

97 HIGH STREET
STREETCAR NO. 625
Columbus Metropolitan
Library
CCVC# 916/H638

98 INTERIOR OF GUY
DENTON GROCERY
STORE
Columbus Metropolitan
Library
CCVC# 272/D415/1920

99 OHIO STADIUM
CONSTRUCTION
Columbus Metropolitan
Library
CCVC# 701/S776/1922/05

100 THE BOSTON STORE
ON HIGH STREET
Columbus Metropolitan
Library
CCVC# 888/L161/1925

101 CHARLES A.
LINDBERGH'S VISIT
TO NORTON FIELD
Columbus Metropolitan
Library
CCVC# 096/L742/1928/01

102 LABORER
SUSPENDED ABOVE
COLUMBUS
Columbus Metropolitan
Library
CCVC# 274/L657/1929

104 VIEW OF THE CIVIC
CENTER
Columbus Metropolitan
Library
CCVC# 882/C582/1933

105 BROAD STREET AT
GRANT
Columbus Metropolitan
Library
CCVC# 883/G761/1931

106 SHEEP SHEARING
Columbus Metropolitan
Library
CCVC# 456/S539

107 ROCKY FORK
COUNTRY CLUB
Columbus Metropolitan
Library
CCVC# 866/R684/1931

108 MERCIER AMPLIFIER
& EQUIPMENT
COMPANY
Columbus Metropolitan
Library
CCVC# 272/M555/1932

109 SOUTHEAST FROM
HIGH AND STATE,
1940
Columbus Metropolitan
Library
CCVC# 890/S797/1940

110 EAST BROAD STREET
PARADE
Columbus Metropolitan
Library
CCVC# 461/E863

111 DESHLER-WALLICK
HOTEL AT BROAD
AND HIGH
Columbus Metropolitan
Library
CCVC# 883/H638/1945

112 RAILFANS TAKE A
RIDE
Columbus Metropolitan
Library
CCVC# 916/R152/1948/01

113 COLUMBUS'S LAST
STREETCAR
Columbus Metropolitan
Library
CCVC# 916/
M224/1948/16

114 DWIGHT AND MAMIE
EISENHOWER ON THE
CAMPAIGN TRAIL
Columbus Metropolitan
Library
CCVC# 096/E36/1952/01

115 FANS AT OHIO
STADIUM
Columbus Metropolitan
Library
CCVC# 701/S776/1952

116 HORSE-DRAWN FRUIT
CART AT CENTRAL
MARKET
Columbus Metropolitan
Library
CCVC# 659/00/00

117 OHIO THEATRE
Columbus Metropolitan
Library
CCVC# 902/O37/1955/01

118 RKO PALACE
THEATRE
Columbus Metropolitan
Library
CCVC# 878/B863/1955

119 CITY HALL WITH
ANNEX, 1955
Columbus Metropolitan
Library
CCVC# 114/00/1955/03

120 DISPATCH BUILDING
Columbus Metropolitan
Library
CCVC# 948/00/1955

Printed in the USA
CPSIA information can be obtained
at www.ICGtesting.com
JSHW072021140824
68134JS00042B/3729